The impossible could not

have happened, therefore the

impossible must be possible

in spite of appearances.

Hercule Poirot

Quote is from *Murder on the Orient Express*, 1934.

Sir Wilfred Robarts
from "Witness for the Prosecution"

Miss Marple

*T*he more bizarre a thing is the less mysterious it proves to be. It is your commonplace, featureless crimes which are really puzzling, just as a commonplace face is the most difficult to identify.

SIR ARTHUR CONAN DOYLE (1859–1930)

Dr. Watson

Quote is from *The Red-Headed League*, 1891.

Believer and advocate of the "faery photograph" craze of the late nineteenth century

Sherlock Holmes

*E*very man builds his world

in his own image.

AYN RAND (1905–1982)

Howard Roark
from *The Fountainhead*

Quote is from *Atlas Shrugged*, 1957.

Allegorical costume for *Atlas Shrugged*

Hollywood scriptwriter

I am the master of a hundred arts,

and furthermore I have

a whole bag of tricks.

Jacob   Wilhelm

Quote is from "The Fox and the Cat," *Children's and Household Tales*, 1812.

Frog Prince

Witch
from "Hansel and Gretel"

15

*I*t was a marvellous sight:

a mighty revelation.

It was a spectacle low,

horrible, immoral.

BRONTË SISTERS
(Anne 1820–1849, Emily 1818–1848, Charlotte 1816–1855)

Anne   Emily   Charlotte

Quote is from *Villette*, by Charlotte Brontë, 1853.

Agnes Grey
and/or Cathy
from *Wuthering Heights*

Edward Rochester
from *Jane Eyre*

Heathcliff
from *Wuthering Heights*

19

We forge the chains

we wear in life.

Artful Dodger
from *Oliver Twist*

Quote is by Charles Dickens.

A Tale of Two Cities

Marley's ghost
from *A Christmas Carol*

23

*B*eauty is not caused. It is.

EMILY DICKINSON (1830–1886)

She was a gardening enthusiast
both in life and in her writings

Quote is by Emily Dickinson.

Many of her works featured themes of religion and death.

All things truly wicked start from innocence.

ERNEST HEMINGWAY (1899–1961)

A Farewell to Arms

Quote is from *A Moveable Feast*, 1964.

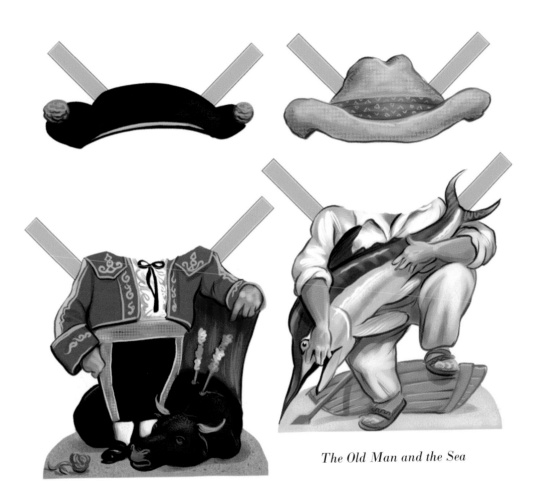

The Old Man and the Sea

Bullfighter

*A*ll that we see or seem

is but a dream within a dream.

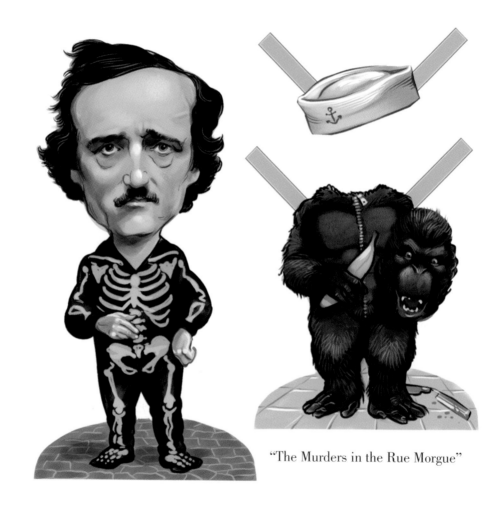

EDGAR ALLAN POE (1809–1849)

"The Murders in the Rue Morgue"

Quote is from "A Dream Within a Dream," 1827.

34

"The Masque of the Red Death"

"The Raven"

*I*f you want to be respected by others

the great thing is to respect yourself.

Only by that, only by self-respect

will you compel others to respect you.

FYODOR DOSTOYEVSKY (1821–1881)

The Idiot

Quote is from *The Insulted and the Injured*, 1861

Crime and Punishment

The Brothers Karamazov

*Y*outh is happy because it has

the ability to see beauty.

Anyone who keeps the ability

to see beauty never grows old.

Franz Kafka (1883–1924)

The Metamorphosis

Quote is by Franz Kafka.

"In the Penal Colony"

The Trial

43

*I*n my younger and more vulnerable years

my father gave me some advice that I've been turning

over in my mind ever since. "Whenever you feel like

criticizing anyone," he told me, "just remember

that all the people in this world haven't had the

advantages that you've had."

F. SCOTT FITZGERALD (*1896–1940*)

This Side of Paradise

Quote is from *The Great Gatsby*, 1925.

The Last Tycoon

The Great Gatsby

What is this world? what asketh men to have?

Now with his love, now in his colde grave

Allone, withouten any compaignye.

GEOFFREY CHAUCER (*c. 1343–1400*)

The Knight

Quote is from "The Knight's Tale," *The Canterbury Tales*, 1483.

Wife of Bath

The Miller

*O*n the whole, human beings want to be good,

but not too good, and not quite all the time.

GEORGE ORWELL (*1903–1950*)

1984 Ministry of Truth

Quote is by George Orwell.

Spanish Civil War uniform from his
freedom fighting days

Animal Farm

What really matters is what you do

with what you have.

H. G. WELLS (1866–1946)

The Time Machine

Quote is by H. G. Wells.

The Island of Dr. Moreau

The War of the Worlds

59

*I*t is better to fail in originality

than to succeed in imitation.

Bartleby, the Scrivener

Quote is by Herman Melville.

Captain Ahab
from *Moby Dick*

Billy Budd

63

*D*ress is at all times a frivolous

distinction, and excessive solicitude

about it often destroys its own aim.

Emma

Quote is from *Northanger Abbey*, 1818.

Sense and Sensibility

Pride and Prejudice

I am. I was. I am not. I never am.

JACK LONDON (1876–1916)

The Call of the Wild

Quote is from *John Barleycorn*, 1913.

White Fang

The Sea-Wolf

71

There is nothing like looking, if you want to find something. You certainly usually find something, if you look, but it is not always quite the something you were after.

J. R. R. TOLKEIN *(1892–1973)*

Gandalf from
The Fellowship of the Ring

Quote is from *The Hobbit*, 1937.

Legolas
from *The Two Towers*

Frodo
from *Return of the King*

*M*an is never perfect, nor contented.

JULES VERNE (1828–1905)

20,000 Leagues Under the Sea

Quote is from *The Mysterious Island*, 1874.

Around the World in Eighty Days

Journey to the Center of the Earth

I can't go back to yesterday—

because I was a different person then.

LEWIS CARROLL *(1832–1898)*

In this
STYLE
10/6

The Mad Hatter

Quote is from *Alice's Adventures in Wonderland*, 1865.

The Mock Turtle

Alice

*A*ll you have to do is to knock

the heels together three times and

command the shoes to carry you

wherever you wish to go.

L. FRANK BAUM (*1856–1919*)

Cowardly Lion

Quote is from *The Wonderful Wizard of Oz*, 1900.

The Scarecrow

The Tin Man

87

*H*e never chooses an opinion;

he just wears whatever happens to be in style.

War and Peace

Quote is by Leo Tolstoy.

The Death of Ivan Ilyich

Anna Karenina

91

It is hardly surprising that women concentrate on the

way they look instead of what is in their minds since not

much has been put in their minds to begin with.

Frankenstein's Monster

Quote is by Mary Shelley.

Dr. Frankenstein   The Bride of the Monster

*B*e careless in your dress

if you will, but keep a tidy soul.

MARK TWAIN (1835–1910)

The Adventures of
Tom Sawyer

Quote is by Mark Twain.

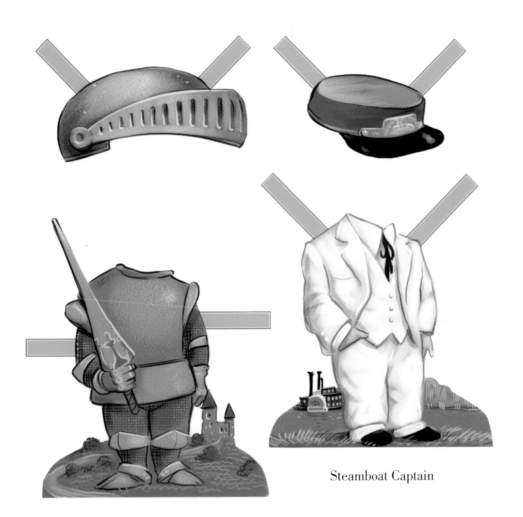

A Connecticut Yankee in
King Arthur's Court

Steamboat Captain

*N*o man, for any considerable period,

can wear one face to himself and another

to the multitude, without finally getting

bewildered as to which one is true.

NATHANIEL HAWTHORNE (*1804–1864*)

Family related to witch
burners in Salem

Quote is from *The Scarlet Letter*, 1850.

The House of the Seven Gables

The Scarlet Letter

103

It is better to be beautiful than to be good.

But ... it is better to be good than to be ugly.

OSCAR WILDE (1854–1900)

"The Ballad of Reading Gaol"

Quote is from *The Picture of Dorian Gray*, 1890.

The Importance of Being Earnest

The Picture of Dorian Gray

*E*veryone is more or less mad on one point.

Shere Khan from
The Jungle Book

Quote is from "On the Strength of a Likeness," *Plain Tales From the Hills*, 1888.

"Gunga Din"

"The Man Who Would Be King"

111

To be what we are, and to become what we

are capable of becoming, is the only end of life.

ROBERT LOUIS STEVENSON (1850–1894)

Long John Silver
from *Treasure Island*

Quote is from *Familiar Studies of Men and Books*, 1882.

114

Kidnapped

Mr. Hyde
from *The Strange Case of
Dr. Jekyll and Mr. Hyde*

*S*ome mystery should be left in the revelation

of character in a play, just as a great deal of mystery

is always left in the revelation of character in life,

even in one's own character to himself.

TENNESSEE WILLIAMS (1911–1983)

The Night of the Iguana

Quote is by Tennessee Williams.

118

The Glass Menagerie

Blanche
from A Streetcar Named Desire

The connection between dress

and war is not far to seek; your finest clothes

are those you wear as soldiers.

VIRGINIA WOOLF (1882–1941)

Orlando

Quote is by Virginia Woolf.

122

To the Lighthouse

Mrs. Dalloway

*S*ome are born great, some achieve greatness,

and some have greatness thrust upon them.

WILLIAM SHAKESPEARE (1564–1616)

Hamlet

Quote is from *Twelfth Night*, 1601–1602.

A Midsummer Night's Dream

Julius Caesar

127